Employee Referral Programs

A Comprehensive Study

Manufactured and published by Books on Demand GmbH, Norderstedt
Cover Design by www.brotz-medien.de

ISBN 978-3-8448-3207-5

About the Author

Mona Berberich (23) is a recent Business Graduate (B.A.) from HFU Business School, Furtwangen, Germany. Her interests lie in organizational management, change and leadership which she was able to explore by majoring in Human Resources and International Organizations. Mona Berberich is an elected member of the City Council of Villingen-Schwenningen, Germany, where she also serves as the youngest Board Member of two city-owned companies. In 2011, she has conducted and published a national-wide study on "Employee Referral Programs" in Germany, whose in-depth research findings serve as the basis of this book.

Dr. Armin Trost (44) is a professor for human resource management at the top-ranked HFU Business School in Furtwangen, Germany. His main points of interest in research, education and consulting are employer branding, talent management and social media. In 2011 the leading German HR journal „Personalmagazin“ ranked him among the top Thought Leaders in HR for the third time in a row. He is author and editor of multiple books and many articles about modern HR and a regular author at Harvard Business Manager. Professor Trost is a well-known keynote speaker at leading congresses about HR and leadership.

1 Introduction

The recruiting process has become increasingly difficult and nowadays even top-companies find themselves experiencing severe problems in finding high quality candidates for their vacant positions. Due to talent shortage and demographic changes the recruiting landscape has changed massively and finding the right candidate has become a struggle for many companies across nations and industries. The time when the classic employment advertising in the local newspaper or in one of the diverse job platforms has been sufficient to recruit high potential candidates has long passed. Especially when it comes to key and bottleneck positions, employers have to seek for new ways to feet their demand for human capital.

'Skill is fine, and genius is splendid, but the right contacts are more valuable than either' (Arthur Conan Doyle, Sr.).

The method of Employee Referral Programs is an internal recruiting method for organizations that becomes more and more relevant in today"s human resource world. The concept relies on the importance of personal contacts by exploiting the social networks of the existing employees in order to find potential candidates for new jobs.

The idea behind it, which is indicated in figure 1, is remarkably simple.

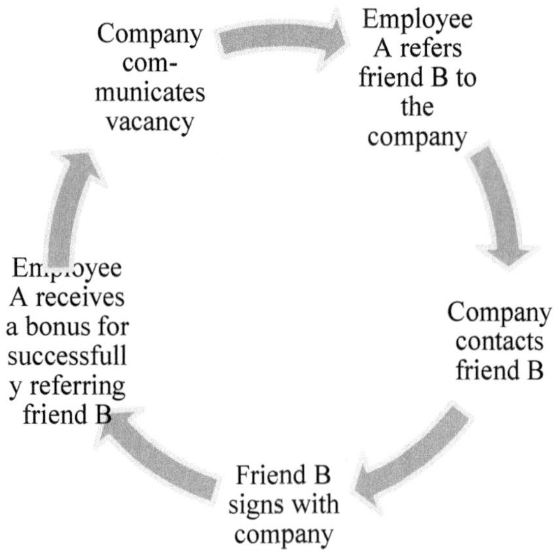

Figure 1: Idea of an Employee Referral Program

In this context, social networks can have positive effects for the new employee in many different stages of the recruiting process starting from the beginning when the current employee turns out to serve as an informal source of information. Likewise, there is an advantageous position for the candidate throughout the actual application procedure and finally after the candidate has successfully been hired. On the other hand, employee referrals and the use of social contacts can also be beneficial for the employer, since he easily acquires a new set of contacts through the employee"s social network which exceeds company borders and is of high quality. Employee Referral Programs and other analog programs are extremely successful and are used by more and more companies in the western world (cf. Trost, 2012). In literature, several reasons are presented to underline those facts.

Up to the present, research on Employee Referral Programs has only been conducted based on test groups and companies in North America. Due to the early stage of maturity of the topic in Germany and greater Europe, there is a lack of research in this area. Additionally, it has to be mentioned that research so far has been unbalanced (cf. Castilla, 2005) and incomparable.

So far, there has not been any research on the number of Employee Referral Programs existing in companies within Germany and Europe as a whole. Empirical data of performance figures of Employee Referral Programs, statistics on levels and type of reward systems as well as success rates in comparison with other recruitment sources are absent. Moreover, most literature concentrates on the benefits for employees while neglecting the perspective of the employer.

This book is an approach of closing the gap in literature and provides unprecedented empirical data of Germany. It is divided into theoretical and practical sections which are followed by a conclusion with a summary of the most important findings.

The theoretical part involves the background of Employee Referral Programs with an explanation of the current level of knowledge and existing theories in literature as well as a demonstration of the psychological background supporting the success of Employee Referral Programs.

In the practical part, an independent study with a sample of large and mid-sized businesses in Germany is presented. Focus of the study is the general existence of Employee Referral Programs in Germany as well as scopes for design and varieties of the programs in terms of organizational form. When analyzing the results of the online-survey, the objective productivity is presented by performance figures and success rates of the existing Employee Referral Programs. This will also indicate the general degree of professionalism of Employee Referral Programs in Germany as well as the level of maturity.

2 Employee Referral Programs

2.1 Nature and Design

Employee Referral Programs or so called “Employees refer Employees” or “Refer-A-Friend”-programs have become an important method in the recruiting process. It is a company‟s reaction to talent shortage and lack of a specialized workforce and represents a new way of recruiting potential candidates by exploiting the existing employees‟ social networks. Employee Referral Programs therefore are not only eligible for those companies struggling to find the right workers but also for those with permanent success who would like to take advantage of their already well-established and highly potential workforce. Companies like Google, Adidas and Ernst & Young are pioneers in leading the charge of Employee Referral Programs. Employee Referral Programs prove to be very active approaches in being able to also reach those potential candidates who are currently not looking for a new job opportunity and therefore do not react to a company‟s traditional employment advertisements.

The general idea of an Employee Referral Program is that the company encourages its current employees to scan their private networks for people who could be potential employees for the company. This ranges from simply browsing through their address books or scanning their business cards to excessive research within social media platforms like Xing or LinkedIn. It has to be mentioned that the hype of social media platforms increases and simplifies the use of Employee Referral Programs. All of this of course under the assumption that high performance employees command of high performance networks beyond company borders (Trost, 2012). If the current employees‟ social networks are exploited successfully, i.e. if a new employee is hired, the referring employee receives a bonus. To put it simple: The company communicates the vacancy of a position – employee A thinks that his former colleague B could be very suitable for this position and refers him to the company – Company contacts colleague B – Colleague B signs a contract with company – Employee A receives a bonus for the referral – Company, employee A and colleague B work happily together!

When it comes to the design of Employee Referral Programs the sky is the limit. There are many different Employee Referral Programs with great differences in style and facets and degrees of professionalism. Differences in financial investments are as extensive as in the hours of devotion for maintenance and further development of the programs. Generally, every company has to define for itself how they can best use an Employee Referral Program and should design it based on their overall goals of recruiting. It is certain that there is no right or wrong when it comes to the design of the program. Each company can let its imagination run wild.

Commonly, Employee Referral Programs differ in the following criteria which will be further explained in the subsequent section:

- Participation
- Employment positions
- Reward system
- Communication
- Technology
- Program evaluation

At first, a company has to define if the participation in their Employee Referral Program is optional for their employees. There is also the possibility of committing employees contractually to participate in the program although this seems rather intelligent since it would ultimately lead to qualitatively lower referrals.

Second, a company has to decide on who is allowed to participate in the Employee Referral Program. Here it is distinguished between simply allowing all employees to participate in the referral process or restricting it for certain groups of employees. Often it is observed that the human resource personnel as well as the management of the company are excluded from the referring process, mainly, since those are the decisive committees within the company. Some programs have a strong focus on recruiting key and bottleneck positions. In this case, only high-performance employees are allowed to submit referrals. The company has then to determine special criteria to decide which employee can take part in the process. Those programs, however, are rare in comparison to the other forms and require high incentives for high performing employees in the first place for them to apply to take part in the Referral Program before they can actually refer someone. In some special cases even the applicant itself is allowed to make referrals while he or she is in the application process.

The type of position for which the Employee Referral Program is used is determined by the main issues the company has. Either, a company can allow referrals for all open positions or it can restrict referrals only for selected key or bottleneck positions which are either of high importance for the company or extremely hard to fill due to a skill shortage in the market.

The most decisive criterion for the design of Employee Referral Programs is the bonus system. As soon as the company has decided if there is a reward system in the first place, type and form of the incentive have to be determined. Who gets a reward and for what? Will the incentive be monetary or in other forms? When will the incentive be given out and in what form? It is obvious that if a person has an attractive incentive to participate in the program it is more likely that the person puts more effort in the referral in order to receive the bonus. Moreover, if a company wants to receive successful and qualitatively high referrals, it is assumed that the employees who participate in the program have to put in a lot of time and effort in order to find suitable candidates to recommend to the company. This is another reason for the company to pay for the service. In addition to that, there is a lot at stake for the employee. He or she has to clearly think about referring a candidate since the impact of negative outcomes can be relatively high. It is an extra task that is done by the employee on a voluntary basis. If an employee has to work an extra hour per day it would normally be rewarded, therefore, it makes sense to also reward this type of work.

The most common types of incentives are financial rewards as well as all kinds of gifts such as weekend trips, i-Pads or even cars. In rare cases, the company offers stock options or non-material compensation such as an „Employee of the Month"-reward. Sometimes, participation in a lottery of all referrals made within a year is offered by the company. The key to the incentive is, however, when and how it will be given out.

While most companies give out the incentive when the referred candidate has been successfully hired, others already distribute the reward after the simple referral or the application of the referred candidate. It is also possible to hold back the incentive until the referred candidate has been successfully employed and completed a certain trial period. Especially when it comes to a monetary reward, the company can decide if the bonus is paid out in a lump sum or in multiple smaller amounts. It is interesting to see if the reward is equal for all positions or different. The company can either decide to make the rewards equal for all positions or give out different rewards for the referral of different positions. In this case there are different possibilities: „The harder it is to fill a position the higher the value of the reward", „the higher the strategic importance of the position the higher the value of the reward" or „the higher the salary of the position that has to be filled the higher the value of the reward". Moreover, the company can determine the value of the reward individually for each individual case.

When it comes to communication, many different scopes for design exist. Generally, the company has to decide if they want to involve an external agency in the Employee Referral Program. If so, when a candidate is being referred by a current employee the agency is responsible to contact the candidate and possibly involve him or her in an application process. On the other hand, a company can simply have the management or the Human Resource Department of the company to contact the candidate in the first place. Sometimes, the company also allows the employee, who has made the actual referral, to approach the candidate and helps him or her with the application process and inform about the position. Depending on the type of relationship between the current employee and the candidate, this happens regardless on an informal basis.

As soon as all the formalities of the program are established ways to spread information about the Employee Referral Program have to be determined. Companies can choose the less expensive way and simply communicate information about the Employee Referral Program via conventional ways of communication like word-of-mouth or e-mail. Moreover, they can include information in the company newsletter or the company magazine or hand-out flyers to the employees and hang-up posters on the black board. However, there are also companies which use special technologies to communicate information and monitor their Employee Referral Program. Here, there are no limits when it comes to design. There are special intranet-tools or even independent internet portals with unique functions and applications. Some sophisticated programs also use social media and active information like Twitter or Yammer in combination with the Employee Referral Program. Again, when it comes to designing ways of communication and technology, the company should ask itself who they wish to participate in the Employee Referral Program. A key account most is most likely not going to see the information on the black board in the factory; the skilled laborer might not follow the company"s management on Twitter.

When the candidate is actually referred by the existing employee, this can sometimes be done by word-of mouth or via e-mail, by downloading formulas from the intranet or by using unique applications of the specially created program website. Generally, it is clear that the better the Employee Referral Program is advertised and marketed in the company the more referrals it will receive. In conclusion, it has to be mentioned that the scopes for design of an Employee Referral Program depend on the resources that are given by the company management.

Summary: Categories shaping the framework of an Employee Referral Program

- Participation
- Employee Positions
- Reward System
- Communication
- Technology

2.2 Methods to analyze the program

If an Employee Referral Program has been successfully established, it is always advisable to use business ratios to measure the success of the program. Depending on how much time and resources are invested in the evaluation of the Employee Referral Program the company may use the ratios explained in the following section.

To measure the overall success of the Employee Referral Program, it is interesting for management in the first place to see how many percent of the people who have been employed within the past 12 months have been recruited via the Employee Referral Program. Consistent with this, the company should determine the absolute number of people who have been successfully recruited via the Employee Referral Program over the past 12 months. To determine the attractiveness of the program, management should look at absolute participation numbers within the past 12 months. If this value is set in relation to the number of people hired, the effectiveness of the program can be assessed further.

Moreover, it always makes sense for the company to look at the cost side of the program. Generally, the overall costs of the program per year should be calculated, defining clearly all aspects of „overall costs". Ideally, companies do not only include value of incentives given out but also labor costs of maintenance, costs of technology and money spend for marketing and advertising of the program. Taking the number of people hired via the Employee Referral Program, the company can establish the so called „Cost-per-Hire" of the program. Again, it is reasonable here to look at those costs compared to other recruitment sources used. Special caution should be devoted to the definition of „Costs per hire", especially when figures are compared in the industry. Depending on the overall goals of the company"s Employee Referral Program, there can be an additional focus on key positions which are characterized by significant value for the company. Here, the absolute number of key positions employed via the program in the past 12 months can be calculated and set in context with the other instruments.

In order to see the significance of the program within a company"s recruiting process, the success rates of the program should be compared to those of other recruiting sources. Additionally, some companies carry out employee surveys identifying the general satisfaction of the employees with the program and consequently collect suggestions for improvements. If evaluations of the Employee Referral Program are successfully carried out on a yearly basis, it helps management to determine the outlook for the following year and establish a general assessment of the program. Likewise, the program can be improved and decisions on further investment can be made.

Summary: Methods to analyze the Program:

- Number of employees hired via ERP / Total of Number of employees hired
- Number of people who participated in the Program
- Number of referrals made
- Overall costs of Employee Referral Program
- Cost-per-Hire of Employee Referral Program
- Number of key positions filled via Employee Referral Program
- Success Rate: Number of referrals made / actual numbers of employees hired through Employee Referral Program
- General Satisfaction: Employee Surveys

2.3 Current State of Knowledge

Up to the present, scientific explanation of Employee Referral Programs almost only focuses on research based in North America, where the topic is much more mature and the use of Employee Referral Programs as an internal recruiting method is widely spread. Especially when it comes to Germany and greater Europe, there is no research based on companies in that area found. It has to be mentioned that the idea of Employee Referrals is only in its early stages in Europe. Only a smaller number of companies have successfully established Employee Referral Programs, many, however, are starting to experiment with the idea and set up pilot programs.

Focus of research conducted in the past was on the benefits for current employees as well as those potential candidates being referred to the program. Many studies concentrate on the effect of social networks for the newly hired employee. Here, the relationship of the recruiting source and the starting salary are in the center. Joe De Varo has found that there is a positive correlation between social contacts and starting salary (cf. De Varo, 2002). The fact that those candidates who have found their way into the company vie employee referrals receive higher starting salaries is also consistent with the positive linkage between inter-industry wage differentials and employee referrals found by Adriana Kugler (cf. De Varo, 2002, Kugler, 2003). Other studies have focused on the relationship of recruiting source and latent job performance of the referred candidate. Zottoli and Wanous have found that those candidates referred by existing employees show better matches and are of higher quality than other candidates (cf. Zottoli, Wanous 2000). In addition to that, Yacubovich and Lup claim that the higher the performance of the employee who makes the referral the better the applicants are who have been prepared for the job by the existing employee (cf. Yacubovich, Lup, 2006). When Manos discusses contacts as hiring channels he explains why workers employed through the referring system should enjoy higher initial wages and longer tenure on account of the better job match that is achieved (cf. Manos, 2006). Casella and Hanaki found substantial reason why firms prefer relying on personal referrals than to hire on the open market (cf. Casella, Hanaki, 2008).

Many researchers including Montgomery have found important psychological reasons why the idea of using personal contacts and therefore the use of Employee Referral Programs successfully works. Yet, it has to be mentioned that research findings have been unbalanced (cf. Castilla, 2005). Likewise great differences in industries and sizes of test groups exist (cf. Zottoli, Wanous, 2000). This ultimately leads to difficulties in comparing different studies. Besides this, scientists have used different definitions in terms of recruiting sources (cf. Zottoli, Wanous, 2000).

When it comes to negative aspects of Employee Referral Programs very little information is provided. In rare cases, the argument of nepotism is mentioned, meaning that people are only going to recommend people similar or analog to them. Therefore, a white middle-class man would most likely refer a white middle-class man which ultimately would lead to a monoculture within the company. This, however, can also be used as a positive argument, since companies can use programs to find special groups of people, i.e. people with special language skills, cultural background or of certain race or gender.

Research of use and scopes for design of Employee Referral Programs is completely insufficient. There is no profound knowledge of numbers of participants of Employee Referral programs, levels of rewards for successful participation and overall success rates within the general recruiting process. Moreover, most literature concentrates on the benefits for employees while neglecting the perspective of the employer. Empirical evidence of existence and performance of Employee Referral Programs in Germany is absent.

2.4 Theoretical Background – Why Employee Referral Programs are said to work

In Montgomery"s 1991 research he described recruiting as a "Social Process" and presents the overriding importance of social ties in recruiting (cf. Montgomery, 1991). According to his theory, workers who are more well-connected might fare better than those who are poorly connected and only possess weak social networks (cf. Montgomery, 1991). Those employees with stronger social networks would therefore have higher chances of finding a better job and receiving more money for it since they could use their contacts to receive an advantageous position in the hiring process. Looking closer, social ties do not only provide advantages in the actual recruiting process but also before and after the hiring. Society knows: „It"s not what you know, it"s who you know". Regardless of what you call it, “Guanxi”, “Vitamin B” or simply “Good connections”, it helps you thrive in the business world.

Assuming that recruitment is an inherently social process in which personal relationships play a leading role, social ties help recruiters to access certain groups of people very easily to which they normally would not have access. Therefore, the company disposes of large networks outside their company borders which can be exploited via Employee Referral Programs. The theories introduced in the following give evidence of the success of those programs.

The Realism-Hypothesis supports the idea of superior flow and quality of information between socially connected people in an employee referral (cf. Breaugh, 1992). When a current employee refers a former colleague or a friend to the company, he or she communicates a lot of extensive and intensive information. Therefore, to a certain extent, social ties influence the flow and the quality of information of the labor market (cf. Granovetter, 2005). A lot of information is subtle and hard to verify. Human beings prefer to receive important information from personal sources which they can rely on. In the case of an employee referral, this does not only count for the applicant who receives information from a current employee but also for the responsible people from the company who receive reliable information from their existing employee.

There is basically a shift in duties when it comes to Employee Referrals. Before the hire, the referrer becomes the actual recruiter and therefore overtakes much time and resources from the company‟s Human Resource Department and reduces the company‟s overall cost per hire. The company has to spent less time on sourcing and screening the applicant since this job has been outsourced to the referrer. Morcover, recommendations by a third party reduce the uncertainty of employees and job applicants (cf. Manos, 2006) which also saves time in convincing the potential candidate.

Employee Referrals provide many advantages for the applicant. A high-performing employee perfectly understands the requirements of the job and the work environment in which the applicant would work and is able to perfectly present this information to the applicant. In addition, the current employee shows much more credibility than the corporate recruiter. Moreover, the employee can test the applicant for possible work tasks and assess if he or she is a good candidate for the position (cf. Yacubovich & Lup, 2006). A candidate who would not fit the position would therefore not apply in the first place (cf. Montgomery, 2001) which saves both the company and the applicant time. In literature, this is known as the "Self-Selection Process" (Montgomery, 2001). Due to this effect of pre-screening, Ullman speculates that people recruited vie Employee Referral Programs are more capable than individuals recruited from other sources (1966, cited by Zottoli & Wanous 2003). Through the information of the referrer, the applicant will also have a clear picture of the company and its corporate culture. The current employee can present an authentic picture in how things are handled in the company, which values are important and which practices are common. This makes the applicant more comfortable and helps him to assess his personal situation much better. In that way, new applicants are tested for their fit not only when it comes to professional capabilities but also when it comes to values and norms.

In conclusion, this realistic view given by the current employee tends to give the applicant clear expectations and will therefore give him or her a more positive attitude about the employment opportunity. It is a massive advantage for the applicant which makes it more likely for him to receive a job offer.

On the other hand, there are also multiple advantages for the company itself, given that the referrer pre-screens the applicant. The referrer in the first place actively forms the employer"s brand image and advertises not only the job but also the company at zero costs. Furthermore, the corporation will receive better and more specific information about the applicant which will give them a more detailed and authentic picture than the one given in the application documents. Moreover, applicants from referred candidates have a better timing (cf. Yacubovich & Lup, 2006). They apply when the market is in high demand. This is not only due to better information about available positions but also due to the ability of friends to motivate each other faster as they have a high persuasiveness. Finally, it is assumed that the company has a positive preconceived notion about the candidate, given that the referrer is a high-performing employee and the relationship between company and referrer is built on trust and commitment.

Given that the Realism-Hypothesis is supported as described above, the Better-Match-Theory also takes effect. Ullmann (1966, cited by Zottoli & Wanous 2003), who assumes in his research from 1966, that jobs which have been gained through referrals present much lower attrition rates than those filled through traditional advertisements and employment agencies. This can be explained by the idea that the employee and his new position as well as the employer harmonize better. Realistic expectations through highly specific information from both sides which is explained by the Realism-Theory together with low fluctuation rates due to a better match can also lead to higher satisfaction (Breaugh, 1992) of the new employee and the company. Given the low turnover rate and therefore many referrals being successful, the referrer should also be satisfied as he or she has contributed positively to the company and his or her environment.

In conclusion, job candidates referred by the firm"s current employees are more likely to survive the selection process and perform well on the job because they possess more appropriate observable and unobservable characteristics and have a deeper understanding of the requirements and the company"s values and norms (cf. Fernandez et al. 2000, Granovetter, 1995).

Another factor that contributes highly to the success of Employee Referrals is the quality of the referred candidate. The Richer-Pool-Theory explains why the referred applicant is likely to be of higher quality compared to candidates from other recruiting sources.

The Homophily-Mechanism (cf. Castilla, 2001) presents an important argument in favor of higher quality of internal sources. Already old proverbs describe it: “Birds of a feather flock together”. It is certain that people tend to know people who are alike, are on the same intellectual level or share the same profession. This “Social Homophily” is based on people‟s preferences to socialize with others similar to them (cf. Fernandez et al. 2000). Research assumes that high potentials dispose over strong and extensive social networks (cf. Fernandez & Castilla, 2001). They are successful which makes them attractive and it is easy for them to socialize and build up networks (cf. Trost, 2012). In conclusion, the employee would most likely refer someone who is similar to himself (cf. Trost, 2012). Ultimately, a company knows what to expect. A high-performing employee is likely to refer a high-performing candidate.

Another argument which supports the Richer-Pool-Theory is the so called "Pre-screening" which takes place before the actual referral is made. The referrer puts the candidate through a very thorough inspection which naturally weeds out all candidates who are not suited for the position (cf. Montgomery, 2001). Through this filter and given that the information which is provided is extensive, the quality of the referred candidate is assumed to be higher. Research argues moreover, that a current employee would only recommend a person if he or she is absolutely convinced that the candidate can fulfill all the requirements which he faces in the new position (cf. Fernandez & Castilla, 2001). Too high is the risk of damaging the referrer"s reputation which increases or decreases with the quality of the referred candidate (cf. Yacubovich & Lup, 2006). This so called "Reputation Protection" also continues after the referred candidate was hired as his work and behavior ultimately reflects to the referrer.

Assuming that the Richer-Pool-Theory takes effect, an important advantage for the employer emerges. As social networks are proactive and match workers and employers even when neither side searches for the other (cf. Granovetter, 1995), employee referrals provide the company with passive candidates. Those "passive" candidates would normally not actively search for employment as it is assumed that they are content with their current position.

Finally, one can argue that employee referrals provide the employer with a steady supply of high quality candidates. Even when the referral does not result in employment, the company has been positively "sold" through the referrer and positive employer branding has been strengthened. If the company remains active and keeps up relationships with those candidates who have not been successfully employed the first time, it can create a "pool" of high quality candidates from which it can draw when new job opportunities open up.

The Social-Enrichment-Theory describes the influence of the social ties between the referrer and the referred employee after he or she has been successfully employed (cf. Castilla, 2005). Hence, it is assumed that the integration of the new employee as well as the whole process of socialization is easier and faster than for those employees who have joined the company via other recruitment sources. There are a number of arguments to support this hypothesis.

At first, the fact that the new employee already has a trustee in the company generally makes him more comfortable. From his referrer, he can receive informal help when it comes to on-the-job training for company systems and processes (cf. Montgomery, 2001) as well as when it comes to establishing social connections (cf. Yacubovich & Lup, 2006). The referrer can serve as an informal mentor for the new employee (cf. Castilla, 2005) who can give feedback and answer question. Given that those attributes are fulfilled, it is assumed that it leads to a positive work attitude and a stronger commitment to the organization which in turn is explained by a lower fluctuation rate (cf. Montgomery, 2001). One could further argue that the reputation protection leads to a higher motivation of the newly employed worker since his friendship is at stake.

The above mentioned theories are in favor of employee referrals and implicate many advantages for the applicant as well as for the referrer and the company itself. Due to those advantages, Breaugh (1981) found significant differences in performance, work attitudes and absenteeism. His Research clearly sees advantages in all fields for those candidates who joined the companies via employee referrals. Further research argues that the performance of the referred candidate increases with the performance of his referrer (cf. Yacubovich & Lup, 2006). This is also confirmed by Breaugh and Starke who argue that informal recruitment sources were linked to more qualified job applicants (cf. Breaugh &

Starke, 2000). The fact that reliability and trustworthiness is established between the referrer and the company, personal recommendations enjoy higher priorities and are key when it comes to filling important positions in the company. This also increases an applicant"s chances. Granovetter (2005) further argues that the well-established social contacts in the firm at the start of the employment serve as a basis of higher productivity.

Summary: Advantages of Employee Referral Programs

- Superior flow of quality and information.
- Reduction of costs and time: The referrer becomes the actual recruiter.
- Better-Match of candidate and employer.
- Steady supply of higher quality candidates.
- Referrer serves as mentor for the new employee.

3 Empirical Study

Employee Referral Programs in Germany

3.1 Problem

The following empirical study aims to provide recent statistical data about Employee Referral Programs in Germany. In order to fill the gap in literature and offer unprecedented figures about existing Employee Referral Programs the issues presented in figure 2 are the main topics of the study.

Existence of Employee Referral Programs

- How many companies in Germany already have established Employee Referral Programs?

Design and Scope of Programs

- How do the programs look like?
- Which are the most commonly used program features?

Communication of Programs

- How is information about Employee Referral Programs communicated?
- Which information channels are used?

Technology of Programs

- Which technologies are used to implement the programs?

Success

- How successful are Employee Referral Programs?
- Which role do Employee Referral programs play in the overal recruiting process?

Figure 2: Main topics of the empirical study

3.2 Research Methods

In order to collect data about Employee Referral Programs in Germany and answer the problem as stated above an online survey was used as the primary method of collecting data.

The questionnaire, which can be found in the appendix, consists of 37 questions about Employee Referral Programs and is designed to be completed by Human Resource or Recruiting Managers of companies within Germany. Participants for the study were chosen out of a population of companies in Germany. The sample is characterized by companies of different industries and sizes. Overall, 479 companies were invited to take part in the study via e-mail. With a return rate of 30%, 145 companies have successfully participated in the survey. The answers of the test persons were received in the period of 30th of November and 22nd of December 2011.

The questionnaire presents itself as structured and closed and was exclusive for those who were invited beforehand. Invitations included a link with an individual password with which the study could be completed online. Multiple voting of one participant was not allowed. The survey contained a set of standardized questions which were presented as a combination of open questions and questions with predefined answers as well as questions were the participant could choose one or more answers within a symbolic rating scale. In addition, the test person often was given the option of adding individual comments.

3.3 RESULTS

The following section illustrates the statistical results gained from the study "Employee Referral Programs in Germany". The descriptive view should help the reader to develop an objective understanding of the findings of the study. From now on, "ERP" will be used as an abbreviation for "Employee Referral Program". Since the questionnaire was designed to provide statistical data in the fields of general existence of Employee Referral Programs, design, communication, technology and success, the following section is divided respectively. All graphs are displayed without the category "I don"t know". All key figures are given for the time period of "the following 12 months", therefore describing the 12-months period from November 2011 on.

3.3.1 Characteristics of Participants of Study

In order to gain a representative view of the population, companies of different sizes and industries were asked to participate in the survey. Figure 1 shows that the sample of the participating companies provides a high variety of industry, there is no bias towards a specific branch. The three industries with the greatest representation are IT-Services, Mechanical and Electrical Engineering. When it comes to company size, the sample also displays great diversity. Whereas the smallest company only employs four people, the largest participating company has more than 220 000 employees. Given the variety of the enterprise sizes, the average company has 1200 employees. It has to be mentioned, that the data of employees always refers to the number of employees the company employs in Germany. With an average company size of 1200, the average staff requirements are 100 employees for the following 12 months. All staff requirement data have been positive and range from requirements for two employees up to 6000 for the following 12 months.

Even though great variation in industry and company size is approved, representativeness of the results of the survey is questioned since the return rate is only 30%. This means that only those companies who are interested in the topic of "Employee Referral Programs" have participated in the survey. However, central aspect of this study was to illustrate how those companies which do have great interest in the topic and already have established an Employee Referral Program implement their programs. For those companies, a predicative picture could be revealed and conclusions can be drawn in respect to how Employee Referral Programs look like in Germany.

	n	%	Valid %
IT-Services	15	10,34	12,00
Medical Engineering	6	4,13	4,80
Mechanical Engineering	16	11,03	12,80
Electrical Engineering	14	9,65	11,20
Telecommunications/Wireless Services	1	0,68	0,80
Consulting	10	6,89	8,00
Vehicle Manufacturing	8	5,51	6,40
Financial Services/Wealth Management	4	2,75	3,20
Technical/Commercial Services	1	0,68	0,80
Biotechnology/Pharmacy	4	2,75	3,20
PR/Marketing/Event Management	4	2,75	3,20
Consumer Goods/Cosmetics	6	4,13	4,80
Taxation/Auditing	1	0,68	0,80
Insurance	1	0,68	0,80
Engineering Services	5	3,44	4,00

Banking	3	2,06	2,40
Whole/Foreign Sale	8	5,51	6,40
Retail Sale	8	5,51	6,40
Personnel Consulting	5	3,44	4,00
Transport/Warehousing/Logistics	5	3,44	4,00
Total	125	86,20	100,00
Missing	20	13,79	
	145	100	

Figure 1: Listing of Branches of participating companies

3.3.2. General Existence of Employee Referral Programs

The central finding of this study focuses on the number of current Employee Referral Programs in existence. As figure 2 indicates, more than half of the participating companies already successfully established an Employee Referral Program. When it comes to reasons for the implementation of the programs, opinions of the participants differ. As graphically shown in figure 3, around 25% of the companies have an Employee Referral Program because they struggle filling important positions in their company. Other companies maintain Employee Referral Programs because they like to try out new recruiting methods or regard it as a way to bind their employees. The remaining 25% maintain their program because it has been successful in the past. From those companies who have not implemented an Employee Referral Program yet, 36% plan to introduce a program in the near future. This can be seen in figure 4.

16% of the companies without an Employee Referral Program, do not plan on introducing one in the future. The most important reason for this is that the companies consider other recruitment methods as more successful. However, as indicated by figure 5, 29% of those companies do show low or no staff requirements as a reason for not implementing an Employee Referral Program.

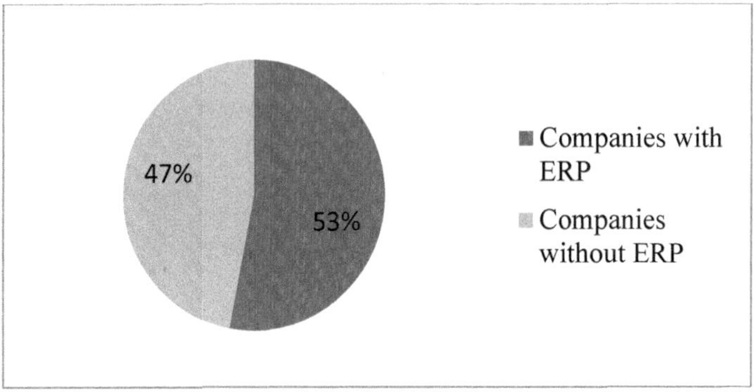

Figure 2: Existence of ERP in Germany

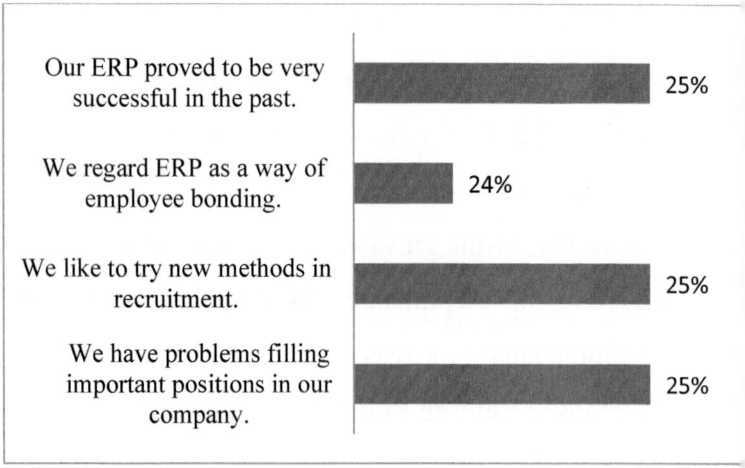

Our ERP proved to be very successful in the past.
25%
We regard ERP as a way of employee bonding.
24%
We like to try new methods in recruitment.
25%
We have problems filling important positions in our company.
25%

Figure 3: Reasons for implementing an ERP

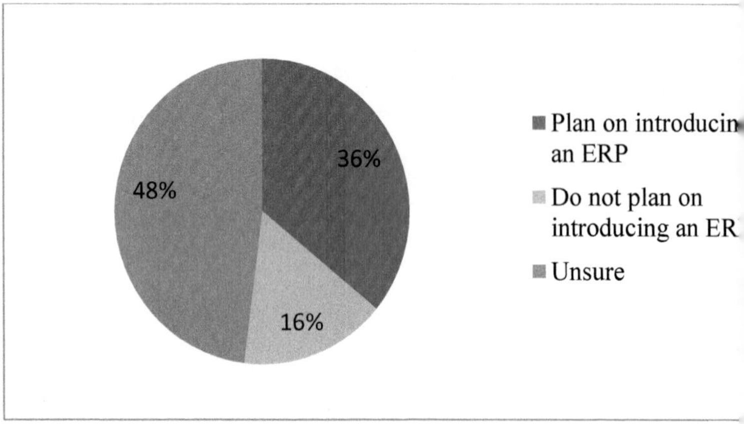

Figure 4: Plans to introduce an ERP in the near future

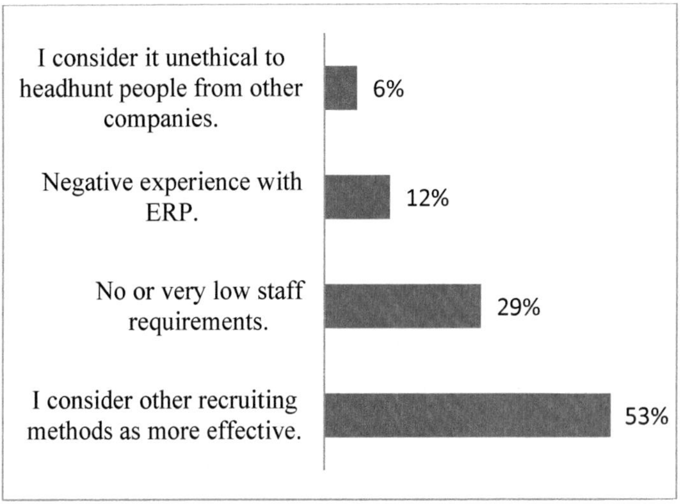

I consider it unethical to headhunt people from other companies.
6%
Negative experience with ERP.
12%
No or very low staff requirements.
29%
I consider other recruiting methods as more effective.
53%

Figure 5: Reasons for companies not to implement an ERP

3.3.3 Design

Within the framework of Employee Referral Programs, the type of participants allowed distinguishes one program from another. The statistical data shown in figure 6 confirm that almost half of the test companies allow all of their employees to submit referrals to their Employee Referral Program. Within 30% of the programs, the Human Resource Department, which is involved in the hiring process, is not allowed to participate in the program. 16% of the programs restrict the management level from participating. Only 1% of the test companies allow current applicants to make a referral. In rare cases, the companies only allow preselected employees to make referrals. A program only for management level has not been identified.

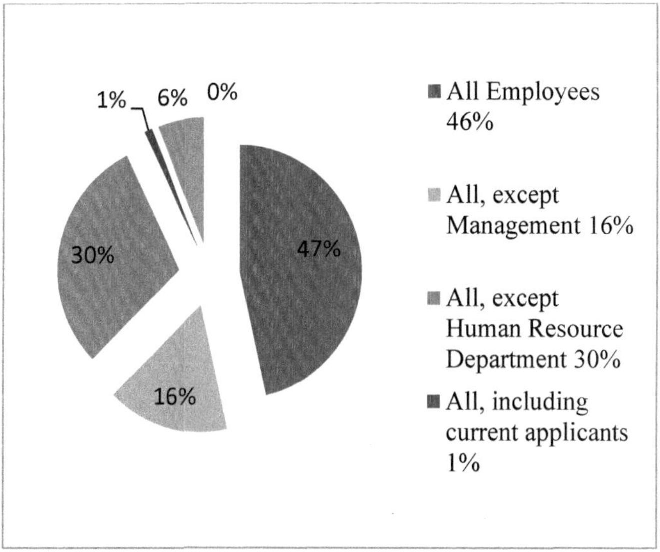

Figure 6: Participants of ERP

In addition to this, 100% of the programs are optional. There are no companies where the participation in the Employee Referral Program is mandatory. Graph 7 shows the positions for which the Employee Referral Program is used, i.e. for which positions employees can make referrals. Whereas 70% of the programs accept referrals for all positions, there is a significant difference in program design to those 30% who only accept referrals for certain type of positions.

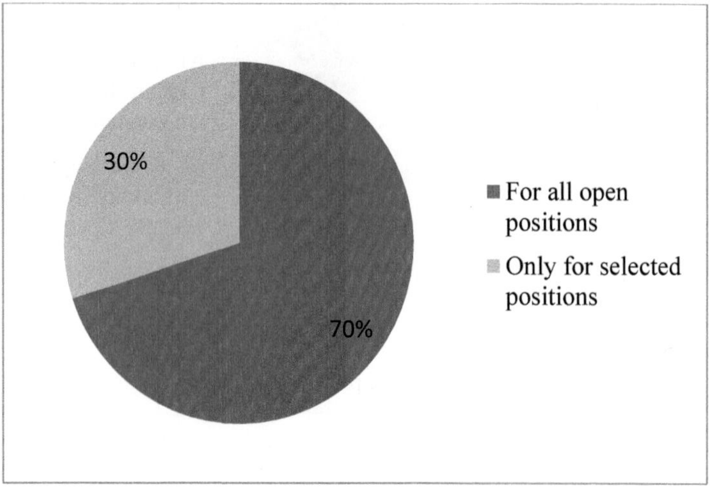

Figure 6: Positions for which ERP are used

Another important characteristic of Employee Referral Programs is the incentive. The survey shows that 94% of the participating companies offer incentives for successful participation in their program as displayed in figure 7. Only 6% operate their Employee Referral Program without offering an incentive. The types of incentives vary. However, figure 8 shows that financial rewards are the most common ones used in Germany. 88% of all companies offer monetary bonuses for successful participation. Other popular incentives are non-cash bonuses which are offered by 9% of the participating companies; 2% offer non-material recognition such as a reward for “Employee of the Month”. Many companies also attract their employees by offering a combination of the above mentioned benefits. 98% of the companies propose a combination of financial reward and non-cash bonus. The most popular non-cash bonuses are i-Pads, i-Pods, gift certificates or a free trip.

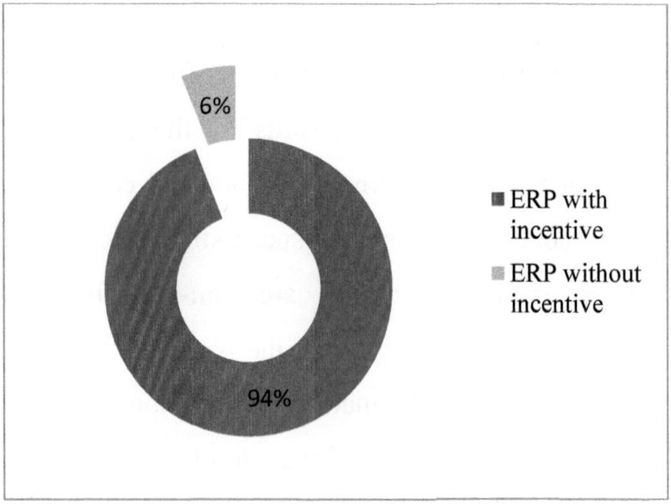

Figure 7: Do the Employee Referral Program offer incentives if participation is successful?

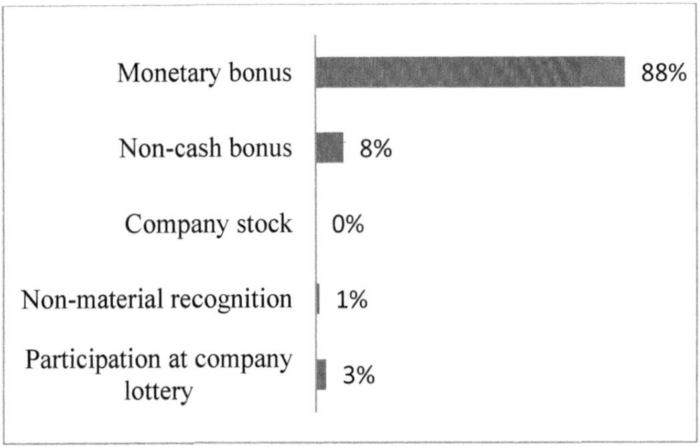

Figure 8: Types of Incentives

In general, within 34% of all Employee Referral Programs the value of the reward varies depending on the position for which the referral is made (refer to figure 9). Here, 43% say that the bonus is higher, the higher the strategic importance of the position for which the referral is made; 33% of the companies offer a higher bonus, the harder the position is to fill. This is further illustrated in figure 10.

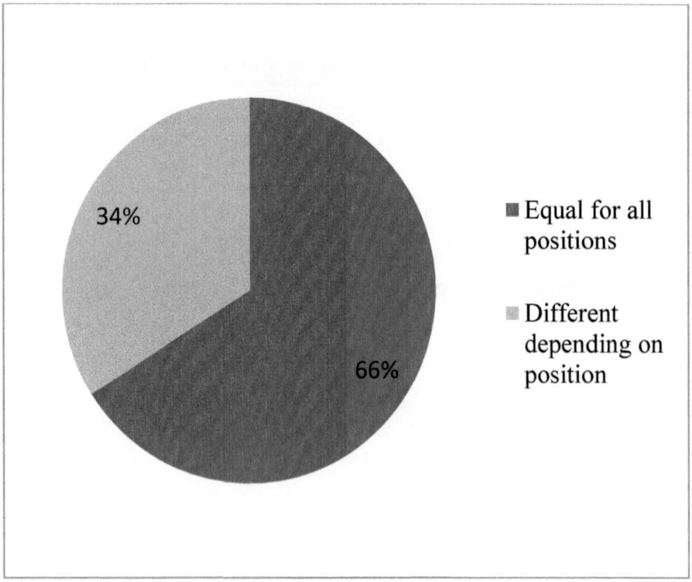

Figure 9: Differences in Values of Rewards

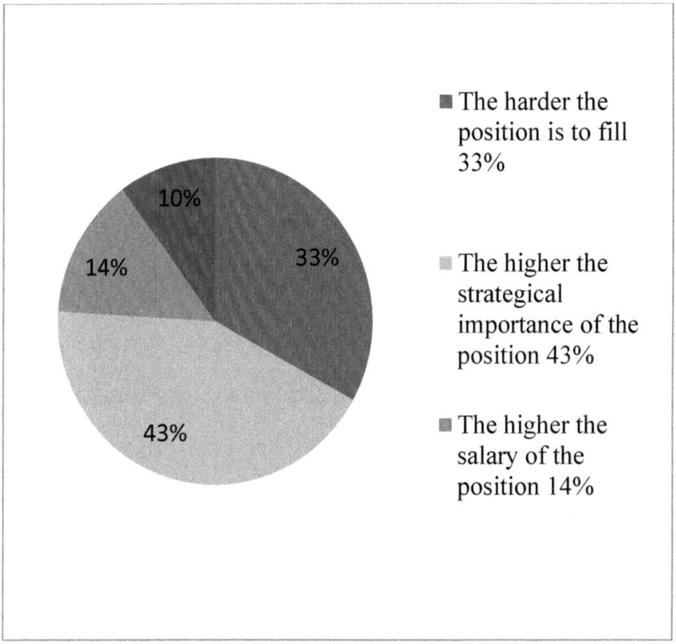

Figure 30: Explanations for Differences in Values of Rewards

The average value of the reward for successfully referring an experienced university graduate is 1500 Euro. In this statistic, the lower 25% of all cases are located below 600 Euro whereas the upper 25% lie above 2000 Euro for every experienced university graduate who has been referred successfully. Whereas the maximum value of a reward is 6000

Euro, the smallest reward is 250 Euro. Acting on the assumption of those values, 85% of all participating companies do not plan on increasing the value of those rewards.

Looking closer at the financial reward, form and type of payment can be determined. As figure 11 illustrates, there are two differences in the form of payment. While 81% pay out the bonus as a one-time payment, 15% of the programs prefer to reimburse the successful participants in several smaller amounts. The point of time when the actual payment is made to the employee also varies. Further displayed in figure 12, one can see that 69% of all companies pay the bonus after the referred candidate has successfully completed his or her trial period; 24% already distribute the bonus after the referred candidate has signed the contract.

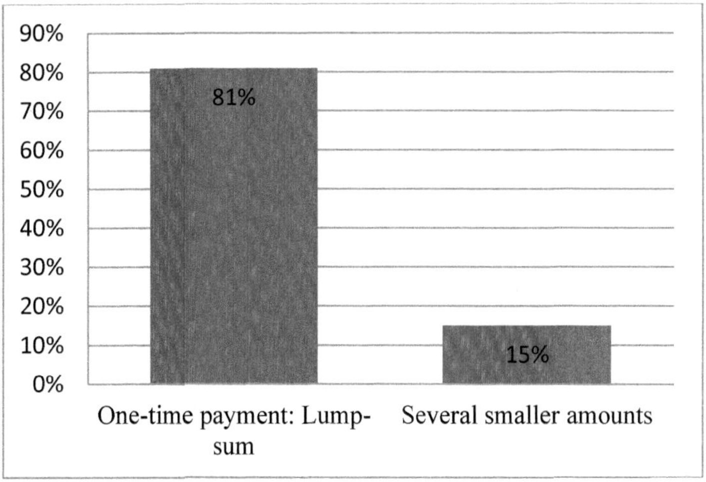

Figure 11: Form of Payment of financial Reward

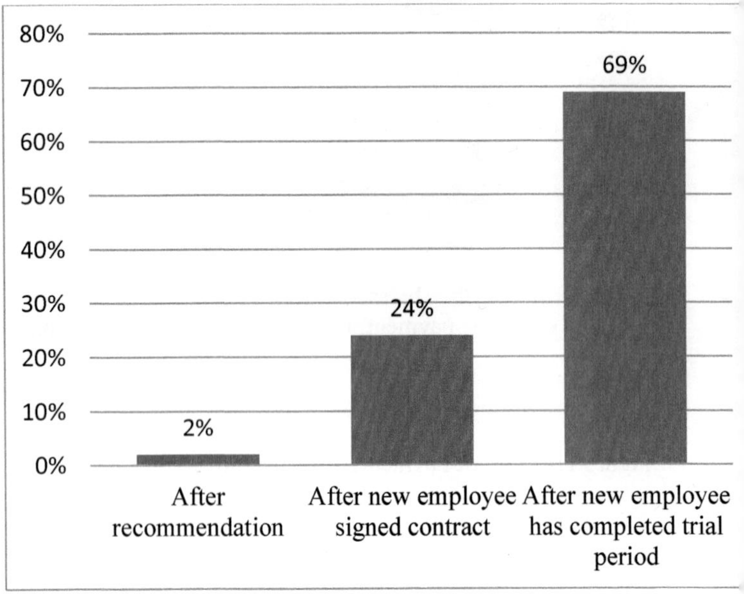

Figure 12: Time of Payment of financial Reward

3.3.4 Communication & Technology

Major outcomes were found in communication of Employee Referral Programs. When it comes to communicating information about the Employee Referral Program, the statistics of figure 13 show that more than a third of the programs promote information via the Intranet. In many companies employees also learn about the Employee Referral Program through internal Newsletters or other classical approaches like e-mail or staff magazines. Only 1% of the participating companies are currently using micro blogs like Twitter or Yammer to spread out information about the program. In addition to that, 26% of the companies use Social Media in combination with their Employee Referral Program. The most popular Social Media used are Xing und Facebook.

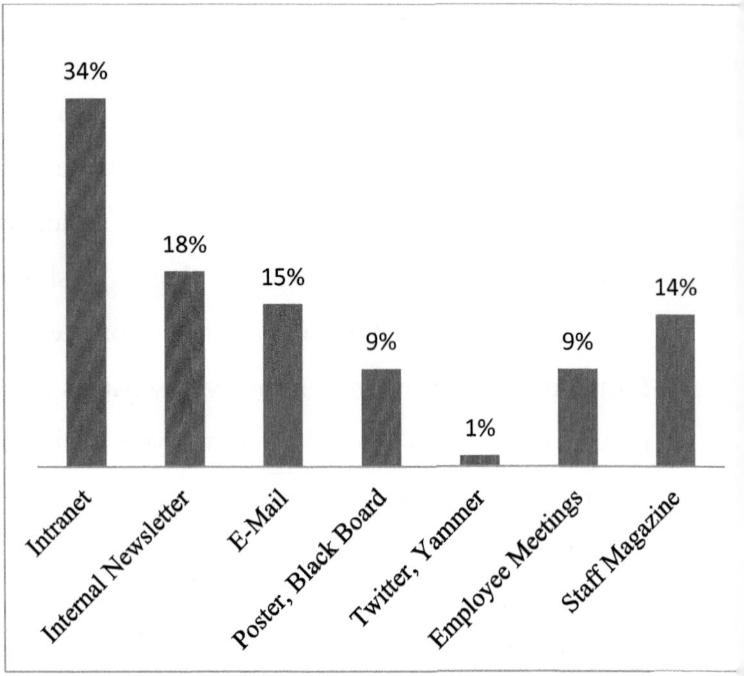

Figure 13: Channels of Communication of ERP

When a referral has been made, the potential candidate has to be contacted from the company side. Figure 14 shows that in 67% of all participating companies the personnel from the Human Resource Department directly contacts the referred candidate. Not one company involves an external agency in their Employee Referral Program. In 25% of the cases, the employee who has made the referral approaches the potential candidate in the first place.

In terms of technology, 72% of the test companies accept referrals through day-to-day communication channels like e-mail or even verbally in a conversation. 21%, however, have already switched to special technologies and applications in the Intranet as illustrated in the chart presented in figure 15.

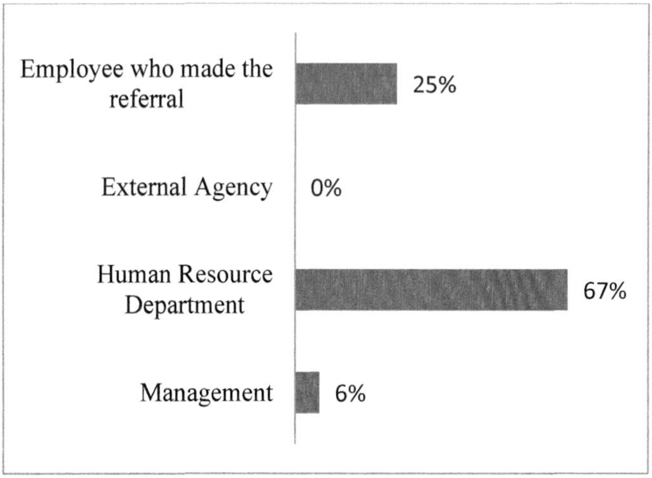

Figure 14: Person who contacts referred candidate

3.3.5 *Costs*

The last section of the survey focuses on the costs of Employee Referral Programs as well as general key figures and success rates. The annual overall costs of an Employee Referral Program have been analyzed in detail. Given that "Annual Overall Costs" includes all costs of the Employee Referral Program such as paid out bonuses, non-cash benefits, labor costs to maintain the program as well as costs of materials, the average annual expenses of an Employee Referral Program are 6000 Euro. 25% of all measured programs show values below average annual costs of 2500 Euro whereas the upper 25% of the programs have yearly costs mounting above 13 500 Euro. The cost-per-hire, here defined as the overall costs per year divided by the number of hires per year, amount to an average of 2400 Euro per person hired. When the costs of an Employee Referral Program are observed in relation to the recruiting costs of other sources, 73% of the participating companies claim that the cost-per-hire of the Employee Referral Program are lower than the cost-per-hire of their other recruiting sources (refer to figure 15).

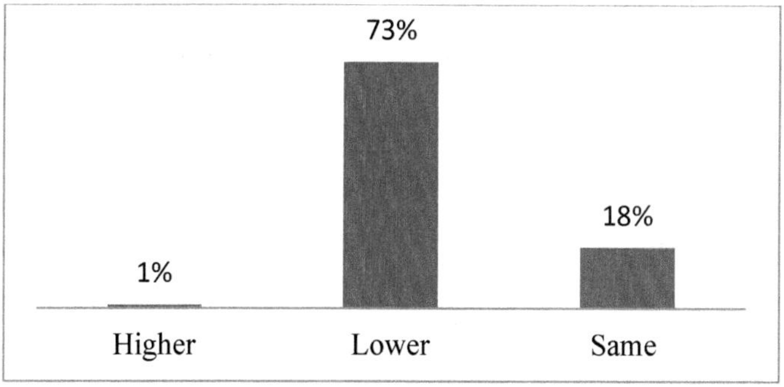

Figure 15: Cost-per-Hire (ERP) compared to other recruiting sources

3.3.6 Key figures & Success Rates

This final section presents the study results concerning key ratios and success rates of Employee Referral Programs in Germany. According to the study, 41% of the participating companies use ongoing business ratios to measure the success of their Employee Referral Programs. Most frequently used ratios are presented in more detail in the following.

A key ratio in measuring the success rate of Employee Referral Programs is the percentage of the newly hired employees, who have been employed through the Employee Referral Program. Here, a company hired on average 5% of their employees, who have been employed within the last 12 months, through their Employee Referral Program. 25% of the test companies hired on average more than 20% of their newly hired employees with the help of the Employee Referral Program. Maximum values of this key ratio go up to 30% of overall hires through the Employee Referral Program. Looking at absolute values, a company with on average 1200 employees hires 25 employees per year through the Employee Referral Program.

In addition to that, the Employee Referral Programs have received on average 25 recommendations to their program within the last 12 months. Here, however, a large discrepancy of the values is observed, meaning that especially large corporations receive much more recommendations then smaller companies. About 25% of the companies receive more than 88 recommendations per year.

The most decisive measurement for the success of Employee Referral Programs is the relation between the number of actual hires and the number of recommendations in the last 12 months. Given the individual success rates, an average value of 3/7 is calculated, meaning that out of 7 referrals, 3 employees are successfully hired.

In order to describe the satisfaction of the company the general attitude towards their Employee Referral Program can be consulted. The study shows that

43% of the test companies describe their Employee Referral Program as an "important instrument" within their recruiting process. This is further illustrated in figure 16. Furthermore, 30% of the companies plan to invest more in their Employee Referral Program in the future. All key ratios can be reviewed in table 1.

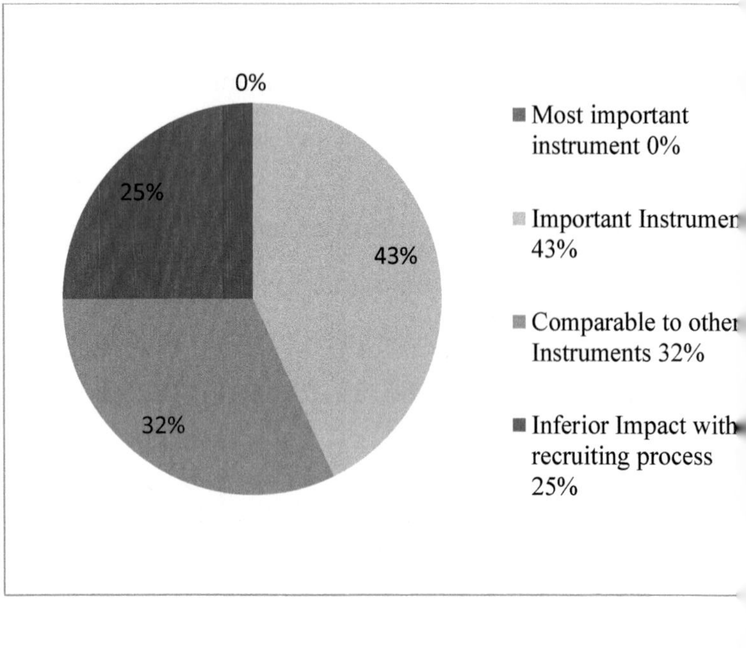

Figure 16: Role of Employee Referral Program within overall Recruiting Process

Ratios	Average Value (adjusted)[1]	1. Quartile	3. Quartile	Max. Value
% of employees hired within last 12 months via ERP	5	4	20	30
Number of employees hired via the ERP within last 12 months	10	3	25	300
Number of recommendations made to ERP within last 12 months	25	5.25	88.75	15500
Annual overall costs of ERP	6000	2500	3500	250000

Table 1: Summary of key ratios

[1] Equals Value of 2nd Quartile

3.4 Discussion

The following part discusses the survey results which have been presented previously and interprets the findings in the context of the recruiting process as a whole. Moreover, general statements will be made about the current significance of Employee Referral Programs in Germany and trends will be identified.

When discussing current number of Employee Referral Programs in existence, the study showed that 53% of the companies already have successfully established an Employee Referral Program. Those companies already have opened up to new ways of recruiting and have looked beyond one"s own nose to get new ideas in recruiting talent. That 47% of the companies have not yet established an Employee Referral Program is because the "War for Talent" has not yet arrived in those companies. Companies who claim leadership in certain industries due to technological advantage or absence of competitors or who are backed up by a strong brand name do not need an additional incentive to attract high potential candidates – not yet. So far, the attractiveness of the company itself has been sufficient to recruit enough talent and allowed to deny the skill shortage. Moreover, 29% of the companies without Employee Referral Program state that there is no or low staff requirements; an argument which delivers another valuable reason for not yet implementing an Employee Referral Program. Those companies were just not forced to come out of their comfort zone yet and try out non-traditional recruiting methods. Due to general orientation towards tradition plus the high uncertainty avoidance of the German culture, it will take much longer until the country opens up to new and unconventional methods of recruiting. This, however, in the long term will cost many talents. The ethical dilemma behind enticing someone away from another company or the thinking that it is “simply not how we do business here” may also still stick in the back of the heads of the company managers.

However, since 53% of the participating companies already have established a program, one can say that Employee Referral Programs are way passed the stage of being just a "Pilot Program". This is also justifiable by discussing the reasons why those companies rely on their program. Here, more than 50% take on a proactive position in recruiting which means that they understand the danger of skill shortage and want to prevent it before it reaches the company itself. Those active approaches also confirm that companies are recognizing the benefits resulting from Employee Referral Programs and strongly believe in their success. Since 25% call their reason for maintaining the program "the past success of the program", it shows that in a large number of companies the Employee Referral Program is already an inherent part of their recruiting process.

Currently, almost 50% of those companies which not yet established an Employee Referral Program are unsure if they will introduce a program in the near future. 16% even say that they do not plan on starting a program. This can be explained since so far there is no research based on Employee Referral Programs in greater Europe and Germany and therefore examples or success rates of other companies are generally missing. This leads to companies having difficulties experimenting with the idea; they have no examples to rely on which makes it hard to prove to management that Employee Referrals are a great idea.

When entering the section for scopes for design of Employee Referral Programs conclusions on how a program can possibly look can be drawn. In general, almost half of the participating companies allow all employees to take part in their program. There is a lot of trust that the company management has in its employees that they will take the program serious and will add great value to the company by making recommendations. There is no difference in groups of employees. That trust plays an important role can also be supported by the fact that nearly no companies allow current applicants to make referrals. At this point, the mutual trust basis is not yet established. Almost 50% of the companies restrict large groups of employees like the Human Resource Department or the management level from the program. This mainly takes place since those groups have a major influence in the decision-making process and therefore could be biased. It is assumed that companies are aware of the recommendations which they are missing due to excluding large employee groups from the program. However, a general belief in the rest of the employees can be concluded from this action; companies trust in their other employees in making sufficient referrals to keep the program successful. That only 6% of the companies limit the Employee Referral Program to a preselected group of employees simply seems to be too time-consuming for management and employees. The incentive is reduced when someone has to first apply to take part in a program where he or she can make referrals. It also reduces trust, since the employee might feel that the management puts him or her through a test first. For other employees, this could be viewed as categorization from the management side and cause dissatisfaction in the company.

When looking at the statistic of optional or mandatory participation, the perfect solution of leaving participation in the Employee Referral Program open to the employees is favored by 100% of the companies. This is easily understandable since the program also enjoys great popularity without forcing employees to take part in it. Not only has management recognized the benefits of the program, the employees also have realized the great advantages that arise when their friends or former colleagues become their co-workers. This is further explained by the Social Enrichment Theory in the first part of this book. Therefore, employees do not need to be forced to make referrals, the incentive of having new colleagues whom they trust is big enough.

That companies do trust their employees and are willing to give up some of their recruiting duties is observed when discussing that 70% of the participating companies accept referrals for all kinds of positions, not just for higher positions or management level. Moreover, in more than 25% of all cases, the company allows the employee who has made the referral to approach the candidate in the first place. Companies, again, value the importance of social ties and are willing to share their competencies. When they allow the first contact by the employee instead of the Human Resource Management they understand that there is a much more effective exchange of information and authenticity than with a person from the Human Resource Department. Likewise, there is no better advertising than when the current employee tries to convince his or her friend to work in the company. The Realism-Theory takes effect on every educational level: Similar people stick together and the employee will refer someone with a similar profession and educational level. Therefore, a company is willing to exploit the social networks of their employees on every level and will not restrict it for a certain group of employees.

Companies are aware of how much work and time it consumes when an employee makes a well thought-through referral. This can be backed-up by the 94% of the companies who offer a reward for successful participation in the Referral Program. Management also wants to remunerate the employee for making the referral so that he or she will continue to scan his or her social networks after already submitting referrals. Working extra hours for the company can be fun if the company values it respectively.

"Money makes the world go round" – a statement that also holds true for Employee Referral Programs. 98% of the companies offer financial rewards for making a successful referral. A financial bonus is the motor that pushes employees the most, regardless of the company level. In addition to this, companies have found another interesting tool in the reward system. Travel vouchers or other material gifts can function as supplemental promotional activities. If the overall process of distributing the gifts is somehow ceremonial packaged, a nice story in the staff magazine or the Intranet does not only push the popularity of the Employee Referral Program it also shows that the company greatly values their employees. Making a big event at the end of the year with a company internal lottery also increases the tension throughout the year and creates additional curiosity for the employees.

Observing the conditions of the reward in more detail one can see that 69% of the companies prefer to give out the bonus after the referred candidate has completed a trial period. In Germany, this trial period is three to six months as a rule of thumb. This can be regarded in the first place as a mechanism from management side, trying to prevent fraud that is done by those employees who see the Employee Referral Program as a way of making easy money. That this is not a sign of minor appreciation can be seen by the relatively high value of the rewards. With an average value for successfully referring an experienced university graduate of 1500 Euro and 25% of the cases with values located above 2000 Euro, the company clearly shows appreciation for the referral of the current employee.

The employees trust is rewarded and through the "Better-Match-Theory", the high reward is also justified. That 85% of the companies do not plan on increasing those values in the near future is a sign that management regards the current bonuses as sufficient to take home great potential candidates and keep the program going. High participation rates and positive success rates also undermine the need for a rise in rewards for successful participation in the program.

Companies value the strategic importance of the Employee Referral Program. This is supported by 80% of those companies who give out different rewards for different positions for which the referral has been made and therefore value referral of key or bottleneck positions exceptionally. In particular, this means that the higher the strategic importance of the position which has to be filled or the harder it is to fill the open position, the higher the reward will be for a successful referral. This also proves that Employee Referral Programs are specifically applicable with key positions, which is also supported by the psychological background "Birds of a feather flock together" (refer to theoretical part of book). Assuming the success of Employee Referral Programs this will lead to a major advantage in a future characterized by "War for Talent".

In terms of communication and technology of Employee Referral Programs it can be concluded that companies within Germany still focus on more traditional channels. When it comes to spread information about the Employee Referral Program, most companies use the Intranet or the internal newsletter. This mostly, since the average person is the easiest reachable through those channels. Never the less, Social Media and micro blogs like Twitter and Yammer have gained massive importance within the last years and companies slowly open up and use those "unconventional" ways of communication to support their Employee Referral Program. There are two reasons, why, however, traditional ways of communication like the company internal magazines or staff meetings and black boards will remain important in the future. In the first place, these classical information channels will always reach skilled labor in the factory best. Second, it always covers those people who have not yet switched to Social Media and micro blogs or are generally suspicious of them as well as those people who do not have access to higher technologies. The low levels for use of Social Media and special technologies for Employee Referral Programs can also be explained by the point that many programs are still in their test phase or in a lower mature phase. In addition to that, since the idea of Employee Referral Programs has not yet gained complete maturity and acceptance, budgets are still limited by many companies. It is always cheaper to go with the already existing information channels before reaching out to new ways, even though sometimes it can be more profitable. The low use of Social Media and other extravagant platforms can be argued with the already existing success of Employee Referral Programs who are communicated through traditional information channels. For some companies, there is simply no need to add additional ways of communication: The program works.

An indicator for the success is given by the key ratios found in the study. The statistic of key ratios that states that only 41% of the participating companies use key ratios to measure their Employee Referral Program can be interpreted in two ways. On the one hand, one could argue that this reflects a low degree of professionalism since the programs are not continuously measured. On the other hand, continuous measurement consumes a lot of time and resources. Many companies do not yet have the manpower and budget to afford much more than the program itself. Likewise, not continuously measuring the program could also reflect that the management of the company simply believes in the idea of Employee Referral Programs. If the company has success with the program and experiences popularity from their employees ongoing measurement is not needed.

The results presented before show many different key ratios which allow discussing conclusions on the overall success of the Employee Referral Programs. All results and key ratios support the success of Employee Referral Problems. Generally, all ratios present moderate but optimistic values, this mainly, because the idea of Employee Referrals as well as most of the programs is in early stages of maturity. However, when looking at the upper 25% of the cases every ratio presents outstanding values. Here, it can be assumed that those companies present the pioneers in recruiting. Those companies most likely have been operating their programs longer and their success is tremendous. Last but not least, because their budgets are higher they can afford more communication tools and technology to support the program.

Another argument for recruiting via social contacts is delivered by the quality of the referrals which is confirmed by the strike rate of 3 to 7. This highly decisive measurement for the success of Employee Referral Programs, here the relation between the number of actual hires and the number of recommendations in the last 12 months, crushes every doubt. On average 3 out of 7 referrals lead to successful hires. This figure is overriding and approves the success of the programs. It appears that the "Better-Match-Theory" proves worthy.

The Cost-per-Hire of on average 2400 Euro seems relatively high in the first place. However, this is mostly due to the high rewards given out. Besides, 73% of the companies argue that the cost-per-hire of their Employee Referral Program is much lower than the cost-per-hire of their other recruiting sources. The costs of the program always have to be assessed in terms of its success. If the Employee Referral Program is successful and generates those benefits discussed before, it is worth the money.

When discussing future perspectives of Employee Referral Programs, statistics for general attitude and satisfaction can be consulted. Not only do 43% of the companies believe that Employee Referral Programs are already an important part of the recruiting process, 79% of the companies also believe that they will play an important role in the future of recruiting. This statistic signals that Employee Referrals are already an integer part of the recruiting process and together with the success rates discussed above will take on an even more important role in the future. Currently, there is still uncertainness and insecurity which results in many companies relying on their traditional recruiting instruments. Highly successful companies are more over sometimes inward-oriented and became comfortable in their comfort zone. However, the direction of Employee Referral Programs is certainly positive and their importance will outgrow the traditional ways of recruiting in the future. All findings discussed above consistently support the success of Employee Referral Programs and strengthen the theories presented by literature. In the future, companies will put even more trust in their employees in finding potential candidates for the company. The use of social ties as well as their importance will increase drastically.

4 Conclusion

The following part will summarize the main conclusions of this book and provides future perspectives of Employee Referral Programs in Germany. Moreover, recommendations for further research will be specified.

The first section of this book sheds light on nature and design of Employee Referral Programs and presents different possibilities of how a program could look like. This gives companies an insight on the idea of Employee Referrals in the first place and can serve as a guideline in creating and measuring a program.

In the theoretical part, the benefits of Employee Referral Programs are illustrated and supported with excessive research about the role of social contacts in business. The psychological background, moreover, conveys why an Employee Referral Program is supposed to work. Benefits of Employee Referral

Programs do not only exist for the job applicant, but also for the current employee and the employer itself. Major findings are the superior flow and quality of information which implicates a realistic view, clear expectations and reduced uncertainty for all parties. In addition, the prescreening mechanism, and therefore the shift in recruiting duties, leads to a higher quality of candidates and a better fit. Due to the Social Enrichment Theory, benefits can also be found after the successful hiring process. Overall positive effects are identified in higher staff retention and greater satisfaction which ultimately results in a strong company built on trust and reliability.

The practical part presents the first empirical study of Employee Referral Programs in Germany. Main objective of the independent online survey was to discover statistical data about the number of Employee Referral Programs in existence and to reveal major characteristics in terms of design and success of those programs. The results of the study rely national-wide on more than 140 companies of different sizes and industries. The survey shows that more than half of the participating companies already successfully established an Employee Referral Program.

Central findings of the study in terms of design illustrate that participation in all programs is optional; most programs allow participation of all employees. No data supports the existence of programs only for pre-selected employees. In addition to this, the programs are used to find candidates for all open jobs; however, there is a special focus on filling key and bottleneck positions. Moreover, almost all companies offer a financial reward for successful participation in the program. The average value of a bonus for the successful referral of an experienced university graduate is 1500 Euro, whereas 25% of the companies pay out bonuses of more than 2000 Euro.

Furthermore, in most companies, the Human Resource personnel take over the communication process. The interference of external agencies is completely absent. In order to communicate information about the Employee Referral Program, popular information channels are the Intranet or internal newsletters, as well as traditional approaches like staff meetings or magazines and the posters on black boards. A smaller percentage of the companies already command over special technologies supporting the program.

Annual costs of the average program mount to 8000 Euro. The success rate of an Employee Referral Program calculated with the results of the study is 3 to 7, meaning that out of 7 referrals, 3 employees are successfully hired.

The evaluation of the statistics was clearly in favor of Employee Referral Programs and allows positive conclusions for their future. In large parts, companies have recognized the benefits of Employee Referral Programs and overcome the skepticism towards new and unconventional recruitment practices to fight talent shortage and the lack of specialized workforce. Not least because of the feared “War for Talent”, Employee Referrals and other active approaches of recruiting will gain increasing importance in the future. It is assumed that companies will put more emphasis on social networks and that investments in Employee Referral Programs will grow.

For further research, it would be interesting to observe the results of this more descriptive study in an international context. Likewise, recommendations for additional analysis of pioneer programs in Germany can be made. In order to gain insight in the current employee"s attitude towards Employee Referral Programs and to explore general levels of satisfaction with the instrument, this study could serve as a basis.

5 References

Breaugh, J 1981, „Relationships between Recruiting Sources and Employee Performance, Absenteeism, and Work", *Academy of Management Journal*, vol. 24, pp. 142-147

Breaugh, J, Starke, M 2000, „Research on Employee Recruitment: So Many Studies, So Many Remaining Questions", *Journal of Management,* vol.26, no.3, pp. 405-434

Casella, A, Hanaki, N 2008,"Information channels in labor markets: On the resilience of referral hiring", *Journal of Economic Behavior & Organization,* vol. 66, no. 3–4, pp. 492-513

Castilla, E. 2001. Working Hard or Hardly Working? The Impact of Social Networks on Employees" Performance. Prepared for Workshop of the Program on the Corporation as a Social Institution, SSRC http://www.irle.berkeley.edu/culture/conference/castilla.pdf (accessed 25 January, 2012)

Castilla, E 2005, „Social networks and employee performance in a call center", *American Journal of Sociology*, vol. 110, pp. 1243–1283

DeVaro, J 2002, „*The Effect of Employer Recruitment Strategies on Job Placements and Match Quality*", Comell University, Ithaca, New York

Fernandez, R, Castilla, E & Moore, P 2000, „Social capital at work and employment at a phone center", *American Journal of Sociology*, vol. 105, pp. 1288–1356

Fernandez, R & Castilla, E 2001, „How Much Is That Network Worth? Social Capital in Employee Referral Networks", in *Social Capital: Theory and Research, N Lin, K Cook & R Burt (eds)*, Aldine de Gruyter, Chicago, pp. 85-104

Granovetter, M 1995, *Getting a Job: A Study of Contacts and Careers*, 2nd edition, Chicago University Press, Chicago

Kugler, A 2003, „Employee Referrals and Efficiency Wages", Labour Economics, vol. 5, pp. 531-556

Manos, A 2006, „The wage effects from the use of personal contacts as hiring channels", *Journal of Economic Behavior & Organization,* vol. 59, no. 1, pp. 133-146

Montgomery, J 1991,"Social networks and labor-market outcomes: toward an economic analysis", *American Economic Review,* vol. 81, pp. 1407–1418

Montgomery, J 2001, „Social networks and labor-market outcomes: Toward an economic analysis", *American Economic Review*, vol. 81, pp. 1408-1418

Trost, A 2012, *Talent Relationship Management: Personalgewinnung in Zeiten Des Fachkraftemangels,* Springer-Verlag GmbH, Germany

Ullman, J 1966, „Employee referrals: A prime tool for recruiting workers", *Personnel,* vol. 43, pp. 30-35

Yakubovich, V, Lup, D 2006, „Stages of the Recruitment Process and the Referrer's Performance Effect", *Organization Science,* vol. 17, no. 6, pp. 710-723

Zottoli, M, Wanous, J 2000, „Recruitment Source Research: Current Status and Future Directions", *Human Resource Management Review*, vol.10, pp. 353-382